D0241614

MARKS &
SPENCER

the eat well cookbook

Marks and Spencer p.l.c.
PO Box 3339, Chester CH99 9QS
www.marksandspencer.com

ISBN: 1-84461-480-8

Printed in China

Author: Fiona Biggs
Cover Photographer: Karen Thomas

Notes for the Reader

This book uses both metric and imperial measurements. Follow the same units of measurement throughout; do not mix metric and imperial. All spoon measurements are level; teaspoons are assumed to be 15 ml. Unless otherwise stated, milk is assumed to be full fat, individual vegetables such as potatoes are medium, and pepper is freshly ground black pepper. Sodium analysis is based on measured quantities within each recipe and does not take into account adding a 'pinch' of salt or seasoning. Please note that adding extra salt will increase the sodium intake in the recipe. Recipes using raw or very lightly cooked eggs should be avoided by infants, the elderly, pregnant women, convalescents and anyone suffering from an illness. Pregnant and breastfeeding women are also advised to avoid eating peanuts and peanut products. The times given are an approximate guide only. Preparation times differ according to the techniques used by different people and the cooking times may also vary from those given. Optional ingredients, variations or serving suggestions have not been included in the calculations.

introduction: a well balanced diet

The cliché that you are what you eat contains more than a grain of truth. However, it must also be said that you are just as much how you eat and even when you eat.

Food providing a balanced intake of essential nutrients and energy, that is calories, tell only part of the story. There are also nutrients in food that help protect against disease and still others that play an important role in maintaining the body's systems in peak condition. Equally, there are some nutrients which, taken in excess over a period of time, can do long-term, sometimes irreversible damage.

And if that's not enough to think about, how and when you eat are also essential considerations for eating well. There is an old saying that you should breakfast like a king, lunch like a prince and dine like a pauper. Research during the last decades, as well as anecdotal evidence, certainly seems to bear this out although not, perhaps, in quite such an extreme form. Schools report that children who eat an energizing breakfast and a well-balanced lunch are better behaved, more attentive and work harder throughout the entire day. Most of us know that if we skip breakfast because there isn't time or we just can't be bothered, then we are far more likely to succumb to the temptation of unhealthy and unsatisfying sugary or salty snacks in the middle of the morning.

We are probably also all familiar with the downward spiral of fluctuating blood-sugar levels and energy levels that is only ever temporarily halted by nibbling a bar of chocolate. Applying the principles of the glycaemic index (GI) diet can help maintain even blood sugar levels throughout the day. Low-GI foods, such as apples, oatmeal and spaghetti are digested slowly, keeping blood sugar levels more stable (and ensuring that you stay feeling full for longer). Medium-GI foods, such as new potatoes, raw pineapple, orange juice and multi-grain breads, are digested more quickly, and high-GI foods, such as pretzels, cereal bars cornflakes and white rice will provide instant energy in the short-term with rapid rise in blood glucose. The key to the diet is to choose most of your food from the list of low-GI staples, and indulge in medium- and high-GI foods in moderation.

What you eat

If all this sounds very complicated and suggests that you have to eat unbelievably boring meals, live to a rigid schedule and ban certain foods, don't despair. That simply is not the case.

The easiest way to ensure a balanced diet is to include lots of different food types and, therefore, lots of exciting variety in the week's menus. Just a quick glance through some of the recipes in this book will quickly reassure you that healthy eating truly means eating well. From Chilli Bean Cakes with Avocado Salsa to Beef Stew with Garlic & Shallots you are sure to find tempting dishes to please all the family. Even kids, who can sometimes be quite fussy eaters, find Banana Breakfast Shake, Tuna Kebabs and Fruit & Nut Squares hard to resist.

All these fabulous recipes are easy to follow with step-by-step instructions. In addition, each one includes an at-a-glance guide to its specific nutritional content with information on the quantities of carbohydrates, fats and proteins, as well as a calorie count per serving. More detail is provided by separately listing the sugar content and amount of saturated fat – watchpoints in any healthy eating plan. To make it even easier to understand the specific nutritional advantages of any particular recipe a symbol guide will alert you to its 'Eat Well' category or categories. The health benefits of these categories are described below.

When you eat

So, you don't have to have a masters degree in human nutrition to eat well – this book makes it simple, rather than complicated. Equally, it is obvious from the recipes that healthy meals are far from boring. It will, therefore, be no surprise to discover that this book also helps you find a flexible way to incorporate a regular pattern of healthy eating into a busy 21st-century lifestyle. The first three chapters provide recipes for the three main meals of the day – breakfast, lunch and dinner – to help you maintain a balanced intake of nutrients to optimize both physical and mental health throughout the day.

Choose most of your food from the list of low GI staples, and indulge in medium and high GI foods in moderation.

A good start to the day is essential for all the family and eating breakfast provides the energy boost needed to get going and re-energize the body after a night fasting. The recipes in Kick-Start the Day are easy to prepare and most are very quick, as mornings are usually a rush for most families. Carbohydrate-rich foods, such as cereals and toast, provide slow-release energy and are ideal breakfast foods. Fruit, too, features in many of the recipes – an easy way to increase the family's intake to the recommended five a day. Light & Lively Lunches provides recipes for quick, easy, wholesome and satisfying dishes to top up the energy levels and keep you going, whether a bowl of tasty home-made soup, a variation on the traditional omelette or a flavour-packed salad. There are even recipes for great light bites to take to work. Desirable Dinners is full of marvellous ideas for the family's main meal of the day – appetizers, mains and desserts – delicious, satisfying and packed with goodness. There has never been a better reason to gather around the table and share each other's news while finalizing the day's energy intake. However, even these ideas are flexible as, although most families eat their main meal in the evening these days, if your lifestyle would work better by swapping Light & Lively Lunches and Desirable Dinners, there is absolutely no reason why you shouldn't do so.

However, life doesn't always run according to plan and there are times when a 'little something' to fill the gap is essential. Consequently, the final chapter, Healthier Treats, offers recipes for just such occasions – delicious but healthy snacks for when you need to eat on the run, when the kids have just come home from school, when the entire family is freezing cold and ravenous after a Saturday afternoon match or when your meeting overran by two hours. These range from quick and easy fruity combinations to savoury spreads and satisfying bakes.

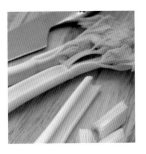

Maintaining a balanced intake of nutrients will help you optimize both physical and mental health throughout the day.

Watchpoints

When it comes to banning foods, many of us are all too well aware that the moment certain foods are forbidden, they are immediately magically transformed into irresistible items of desire. This is why the emphasis throughout Eat Well is on healthy balance including fabulous, flavour-packed, nutritional ingredients rather than avoiding specific food groups. That said, there is no denying that modern research has demonstrated that certain products can be quite harmful, especially if eaten to excess.

Eating fruit need not be boring - check out our delicious Vitality Boosters for healthy snacks on the run.

Nowadays, most people are aware that the Western diet tends to contain too much fat and that the type that really does the damage is saturated fat, which usually comes from animal sources. A diet with a disproportionate amount of fat can make you gain weight, if there is a high proportion of saturated fat, it can increase blood cholesterol and the risk of heart disease. This is as serious for children as it is for adults, and can establish an unhealthy pattern of eating for life. Following the recipes in Eat Well is an easy way to ensure that none of the family is eating too much fat and, equally important, that everyone is getting the right amount of 'good' fats. In addition, for those who think they may have been a little too generous with the fats in the past, there are a number of low-fat recipes to help launch your healthy eating plan.

Sugar is another temptation that is hard to resist and, of course, the occasional sweet treat will cause no real harm. Although sugar is a source of calories there are no other nutrients. It is also bad for the teeth. Consuming sugar provides a sudden energy surge, followed soon after by an equally abrupt dip in energy. The natural sugar found in fruit is broken down more slowly than processed or refined sugar as it comes 'packaged' with nutrients which helps the body to process it. Instead of providing the body with vitamins and minerals, refined sugar actually uses up precious micro-nutrients to process it. Turn to the sweet recipes in Eat Well, most of them based on fresh or dried fruit and all of them delicious.

High levels of salt in the diet are thought to be associated with high blood pressure and increased risk of stroke. Salt can be cleverly substituted in other ways – additional flavour can be added through using spicy marinades and sprinkling the cooked dish with fresh herbs and in doing this no-one will even notice the much lower or even non-existent salt level. And, of course, when you are in charge of the cooking, you are also fully in control of how much or how little salt you add.

Sensible guidelines, such as eating only moderate amounts of dairy foods, are not always easy to follow – how much is moderate and is it the same amount when applied to double cream as low-fat yogurt? Eat Well has been compiled in line with modern nutritional recommendations and provides easily accessible nutritional data, so you don't have to give yourself a headache trying to find the answers to such questions.

Eat Well categories

These categories highlight special features in the recipes, from specific ingredients that are particularly beneficial to health, to low levels of ingredients that are not or, at least, not if eaten in excess. Many of the recipes fall into a number of categories, demonstrating just how easy it is to eat well.

Some categories, such as low-fat, are self-explanatory. You can check the exact fat content – both saturated and unsaturated – in the nutritional information of each flagged recipe. Recipes are assigned a 'Low-Fat' icon (see icons, below right) if they contain 3g of fat or less per serving. Other categories may be vaguely familiar, but slightly puzzling.

The five-a-day category refers to fruit and vegetables, which are highly nutritious and very rich in vitamins and minerals. They contain very little fat, few calories and are often a good source of fibre. In addition, many contain naturally occurring chemicals that may help to protect against such diseases as cancer and heart disease. 'Five a Day' icons are given to any recipes which contribute to the recommended daily intake of five pieces of fruit and vegetables. One serving of fruit or vegetables is considered to be 80g and any contribution to the daily recommendation is marked with an icon.

Omega-3 is a 'good' fat and, in fact, it helps maintain a strong and healthy heart and circulatory system. The National Institute of Health recommends that people consume at least 2% of their total daily calories as Omega-3 fats. The Omega-3 icon appears against any recipe that contains foods which contribute to the advised intake. These are foods are polyunsaturated essential fatty acids and Omega-3 can be found in flaxseeds and walnuts, soybeans, navy beans, or kidney beans, tofu, fish, winter squash, and olive oil.

The Glycaemic Index rates carbohydrate foods from 100 to 0 and measures the rise in blood sugar levels that is caused by each one. All foods are compared to the effect pure glucose has on blood glucose which is given an arbitrary figure of 100. Low GI foods take longer to absorb and keep blood sugar levels more constant. Low GI foods are considered to be below 55 on this scale and are marked with an icon.

the eat well categories

 5 a day

 omega-3

 low-fat

 low GI

kick start the day

citrus zing

prepare in 10 mins
cooking time 0 mins
serves 4

ingredients
1 pink grapefruit
1 yellow grapefruit
3 oranges

1 Using a sharp knife, carefully cut away all the peel and pith from the grapefruit and oranges.

2 Working over a bowl to catch the juice, carefully cut the grapefruit and orange segments between the membranes to obtain skinless segments of fruit. Discard any pips. Add the segments to the bowl and gently mix together. Cover and refrigerate until required or divide between 4 serving dishes and serve immediately.

Calories 84kcal	Fat 0.24g
Protein 2.4g	Saturates 0.00g
Carbohydrate 19.2g	Fibre 3.78g
Sugar 19.2g	Salt 0.03g

banana breakfast shake

1 Put the bananas, yogurt, milk, and vanilla essence into a food processor and process until smooth.

2 Serve at once.

prepare in 5 mins

cooking time 0 mins

serves 2

ingredients

2 ripe bananas

200 ml/7 fl oz low-fat
  natural yogurt

125 ml/4 fl oz skimmed milk

$^{1}/_{2}$ tsp vanilla essence

Calories 262kcal	Fat 1.5g
Protein 8.5g	Saturates 0.9g
Carbohydrate 57.1g	Fibre 1.3g
Sugar 34.9g	Salt 0.24g

five a day

prepare in 10 mins
cooking time 0 mins
serves 2

ingredients

24 CARROT
handful of cracked ice
2 carrots, coarsely chopped
115 g/4 oz canned pineapple
pieces in juice, drained
175 ml/6 fl oz pineapple juice,
chilled
cucumber slices, to decorate

IN THE PINK
1 blood orange
5-cm/2-in piece of cucumber,
peeled and cut into chunks
300 ml/10 fl oz tomato juice, chilled
dash of Worcestershire sauce
cucumber slices, to decorate

ON THE BEET
175 g/6 oz cooked beetroot, chopped
125 ml/4 fl oz orange juice, chilled
5 tbsp natural yogurt, chilled
150 ml/5 fl oz still mineral water,
chilled
orange slices, to decorate

1 To make the 24 CARROT, put the ice into the blender, add the carrots, pineapple pieces and pineapple juice and process until slushy. Pour into chilled glasses, decorate with cucumber slices and serve with straws.

2 To make the IN THE PINK, peel the orange, removing all traces of white pith. Holding it over a plate to catch the juice, cut out the segments from the membranes. Squeeze the membranes over the plate to extract any juice. Place the segments and the juice in the blender. Add the cucumber and tomato juice and season to taste with Worcestershire sauce. Process at high speed, then strain into chilled glasses and serve, decorated with cucumber slices.

3 To make the ON THE BEET, put the beetroot, orange juice, yogurt and water into the blender. Process until smooth, then pour into chilled glasses and serve, decorated with orange slices.

Calories 91kcal	Fat 0.33g
Protein 0.9g	Saturates 0.08g
Carbohydrate 22.5g	Fibre 2.21g
Sugar 22.1g	Salt 0.07g

porridge

1 Heat the water in a saucepan until boiling and pour in the oats, stirring continuously.

2 Allow to return to the boil and continue to stir for 2–3 minutes (or according to the packet instructions).

3 Add salt or sugar to taste and serve at once in a warm bowl. The nutritional information below is based on no sugar having been added.

prepare in 5 mins
cooking time 10 – 15 mins
serves 1

ingredients
300 ml/10 fl oz water
40 g/1 1/2 oz coarse oats
salt

Calories 160kcal	Fat 3.48g
Protein 5.0g	Saturates 0.00g
Carbohydrate 29.1g	Fibre 2.72g
Sugar 0.0g	Salt 0.09g

exotic dried fruit compote

prepare in 5 mins
cooking time 15 mins
serves 4

ingredients

115 g/4 oz no-soak dried peaches

85 g/3 oz no-soak dried apricots

55 g/2 oz no-soak dried pineapple
chunks

55 g/2 oz no-soak dried mango
slices

225 ml/8 fl oz unsweetened clear
apple juice

4 tbsp low-fat natural yogurt
(optional)

1 Put the dried fruit into a small saucepan with the apple juice. Bring slowly to the boil, then reduce the heat to low, cover and simmer for 10 minutes.

2 Spoon into serving dishes and top each serving with a tablespoon of yogurt, if desired. Serve immediately.

Calories 165kcal	Fat 0.92g
Protein 5.1g	Saturates 0.26g
Carbohydrate 36.6g	Fibre 4.85g
Sugar 36.5g	Salt 0.09g

fresh fruit muesli

prepare in 5 mins
cooking time 0 mins
serves 1

ingredients

115 g/4 oz fresh fruit
(e.g. apples, strawberries,
peaches, apricots)
1 tbsp porridge oats, pre-soaked
1 tbsp water
1 tsp chopped hazelnuts

1 Wash the fresh fruit and trim as necessary. Chop or slice.

2 Mix in the cereal base and water.

3 Sprinkle with chopped hazelnuts.

Calories 129kcal	Fat 4.6g
Protein 3.4g	Saturates 0.2g
Carbohydrate 19.8g	Fibre 4.36g
Sugar 8.8g	Salt 0.02g

bircher muesli

1 Put the oats and apple juice into a mixing bowl and combine well. Cover and refrigerate overnight.

2 To serve, stir the apple and yogurt into the soaked oats and divide between 4 serving bowls. Top with the blackberries and plums.

prepare in 5 mins + 8 hrs soaking

cooking time 0 mins

serves 4

ingredients

150 g/5¹/₂ oz rolled oats

225 ml/8 fl oz apple juice

1 apple, grated

125 ml/4 fl oz natural yogurt

150 g/5¹/₂ oz blackberries

2 plums, stoned and sliced

Calories 217kcal	Fat 3.8g
Protein 6.8g	Saturates 0.2g
Carbohydrate 41.7g	Fibre 4.6g
Sugar 14.4g	Salt 0.09g

greek yogurt with honey, nuts & blueberries

ingredients

3 tbsp clear honey

80 g/3 oz mixed unsalted nuts

8 tbsp low-fat Greek Yogurt

200 g/7 oz fresh blueberries

1 Heat the honey in a small saucepan over a medium heat, add the nuts and stir until they are well coated. Remove from the heat and leave to cool slightly.

2 Divide the yogurt between 4 serving bowls, then spoon over the nut mixture and blueberries.

Calories 231kcal	Fat 11.7g
Protein 8.9g	Saturates 2.1g
Carbohydrate 24.1g	Fibre 1.6g
Sugar 1.0g	Salt 0.3g

scrambled eggs with smoked salmon

1 Break the eggs into a large bowl and whisk together with the milk and dill. Season to taste with salt and pepper. Add the smoked salmon and mix to combine.

2 Melt the butter in a large non-stick frying pan and pour in the egg and smoked salmon mixture. Using a wooden spatula, gently scrape the egg away from the sides of the pan as it begins to set and swirl the pan slightly to allow the uncooked egg to fill the surface.

3 When the eggs are almost cooked but still creamy, remove from the heat and spoon on the prepared toast, if using. Serve immediately, garnished with a sprig of dill.

prepare in 10 mins
cooking time 5 mins
serves 4

ingredients

4 eggs
90 ml/3 fl oz semi-skimmed milk
2 tbsp chopped fresh dill, plus
    extra for garnishing
salt and pepper
50 g/1¹/₂ oz smoked salmon,
    cut into small pieces
15 g/¹/₂ oz butter
slices rustic bread, toasted (optional)

Calories 148kcal   Fat 10.6g

Protein 12.3g   Saturates 4.2g

Carbohydrate 1.1g   Fibre 0.1g

Sugar 1.1g   Salt 1.0g

asparagus with poached eggs & parmesan

prepare in 10 mins
cooking time 10 mins
serves 4

ingredients

300 g/10^1/$_2$ oz asparagus,
trimmed
4 large eggs
60 g/2 oz Parmesan cheese
pepper

1 Bring 2 saucepans of water to the boil. Add the asparagus to 1 saucepan, return to a simmer and cook for 5 minutes, or until just tender.

2 Meanwhile, reduce the heat of the second saucepan to a simmer and carefully crack in the eggs, one at a time. Poach for 3 minutes, or until the whites are just set but the yolks are still soft. Remove with a slotted spoon.

3 Drain the asparagus and divide between 4 warmed plates. Top each plate of asparagus with an egg and shave over the cheese. Season to taste with pepper and serve immediately.

Calories 169kcal	Fat 11.3g
Protein 15.2g	Saturates 4.6g
Carbohydrate 1.6g	Fibre 1.3g
Sugar 1.5g	Salt 0.48g

tuscan beans on ciabatta toast with fresh herbs

1 Heat the oil in a medium sauté pan and cook the onion over a low heat until soft. Add the garlic and cook for a further 1 minute, then add the butter beans, water and tomato purée. Bring to the boil, stirring occasionally, and cook for 2 minutes.

2 Add the balsamic vinegar, parsley and basil and stir to combine. Season to taste with pepper and serve over slices of toasted ciabatta.

prepare in 5 mins
cooking time 10 mins
serves 2

ingredients
1 tbsp olive oil
1 small onion, finely diced
1 garlic clove, crushed
250 g/9 oz canned butter beans,
   drained and rinsed
90 ml/3 fl oz water
1 tbsp tomato purée
1 tsp balsamic vinegar
1 tbsp chopped fresh parsley
1 tbsp torn fresh basil
pepper
TO SERVE
slices ciabatta bread, toasted

Calories 370kcal	Fat 9.2g
Protein 14.9g	Saturates 1.3g
Carbohydrate 60.5g	Fibre 6.8g
Sugar 6.8g	Salt 1.18g

baked eggs with spinach

prepare in 10 mins
cooking time 30 mins
serves 4

ingredients

1 tbsp olive oil

3 shallots, finely chopped

500 g/1 lb 2 oz baby spinach leaves

4 tbsp skimmed milk

freshly grated nutmeg

pepper

4 large eggs

2 tbsp Parmesan cheese,

finely grated

TO SERVE

toasted granary bread

1 Preheat the oven to 200°C/400°F/Gas Mark 6. Heat the oil in a frying pan over a medium heat, add the shallots and cook, stirring frequently, for 4–5 minutes, or until soft. Add the spinach, cover and cook for 2–3 minutes, or until the spinach has wilted. Remove the lid and cook until all the liquid has evaporated.

2 Add the cream to the spinach and season to taste with nutmeg and pepper. Spread the spinach mixture over the base of a shallow gratin dish and make 4 wells in the mixture with the back of a spoon.

3 Crack an egg into each well and scatter over the cheese. Bake in the preheated oven for 12–15 minutes, or until the eggs are set. Serve with toasted granary bread.

Calories 188kcal	Fat 12.5g
Protein 14.6g	Saturates 3.5g
Carbohydrate 4.5g	Fibre 2.9g
Sugar 3.8g	Salt 0.8g

light & lively lunches

winter warmer red lentil soup

prepare in 15 mins
cooking time 40 mins
serves 6

ingredients

225 g/8 oz dried red split lentils

1 red onion, diced

2 large carrots, sliced

1 celery stick, sliced

1 parsnip, diced

1 garlic clove, crushed

1.2 litres/2 pints vegetable stock

2 tsp paprika

freshly ground black pepper

1 tbsp snipped fresh chives,
to garnish

TO SERVE

6 tbsp low-fat natural fromage
frais (optional)

crusty wholemeal or white bread

1 Put the lentils, onion, vegetables, garlic, stock and paprika into a large saucepan. Bring to the boil and boil rapidly for 10 minutes. Reduce the heat, cover and simmer for 20 minutes, or until the lentils and vegetables are tender.

2 Leave the soup to cool slightly, then purée in small batches in a food processor or blender. Process until the mixture is smooth.

3 Return the soup to the saucepan and heat through thoroughly. Season to taste with pepper.

4 To serve, ladle the soup into warmed bowls and swirl in a tablespoonful of fromage frais, if desired. Sprinkle the chives over the soup to garnish and serve immediately with crusty bread.

Calories 176kcal	Fat 1.6g
Protein 10.6g	Saturates 0.21g
Carbohydrate 31.7g	Fibre 4.92g
Sugar 7.8g	Salt 0.72g

speedy broccoli soup

1 Cut the broccoli into florets and set aside. Cut the thicker broccoli stalks into 1-cm/^{1}/$_2$-inch dice and put into a large saucepan with the leek, celery, garlic, potato, stock and bay leaf. Bring to the boil, then reduce the heat, cover and simmer for 15 minutes.

2 Add the broccoli florets to the soup and return to the boil. Reduce the heat, cover and simmer for a further 3–5 minutes, or until the potato and broccoli stalks are tender.

3 Remove from the heat and leave the soup to cool slightly. Remove and discard the bay leaf. Purée the soup, in small batches, in a food processor or blender until smooth.

4 Return the soup to the saucepan and heat through thoroughly. Season to taste with pepper. Ladle the soup into warmed bowls and serve immediately with crusty bread or toasted croûtons.

prepare in 10 mins

cooking time 30 mins

serves 6

ingredients

350 g/12 oz broccoli

1 leek, sliced

1 celery stick, sliced

1 garlic clove, crushed

350 g/12 oz potato, diced

1 litre/1^3/$_4$ pints vegetable stock

1 bay leaf

freshly ground black pepper

TO SERVE

crusty bread or toasted
   croûtons (optional)

Calories 86kcal	Fat 1.3g
Protein 4.9g	Saturates 0.15g
Carbohydrate 14.6g	Fibre 2.89g
Sugar 2.0g	Salt 1.09g

fluffy prawn omelette

prepare in 10 mins
cooking time 10 mins
serves 2 – 4

ingredients

115 g/4 oz cooked peeled
prawns, thawed if frozen
4 spring onions, chopped
55 g/2 oz courgette, grated
4 eggs, separated
few dashes of Tabasco sauce,
to taste
3 tbsp milk
pepper
1 tbsp sunflower or olive oil
25 g/1 oz mature Cheddar
cheese, grated

1 Pat the prawns dry with kitchen paper, then mix with the spring onions and courgette in a bowl and reserve.

2 Using a fork, beat the egg yolks with the Tabasco, milk and pepper to taste in a separate bowl.

3 Whisk the egg whites in a large bowl until stiff, then gently stir the egg yolk mixture into the egg whites, taking care not to over-mix.

4 Heat the oil in a large, non-stick frying pan and when hot pour in the egg mixture. Cook over a low heat for 4–6 minutes, or until lightly set. Preheat the grill.

5 Spoon the prawn mixture on top of the eggs and sprinkle with the cheese. Cook under the preheated grill for 2–3 minutes, or until set and the top is golden brown. Cut into wedges and serve immediately.

Calories 179kcal	Fat 12.0g
Protein 16.7g	Saturates 3.8g
Carbohydrate 1.1g	Fibre 0.3g
Sugar 1.1g	Salt 1.51g

broccoli & sesame frittata

1 Cook the broccoli in a saucepan of lightly salted boiling water for 4 minutes. Add the asparagus after 2 minutes. Drain, then plunge into cold water. Drain again and reserve.

2 Heat the oil in a large frying pan over a low heat, add the onion, garlic and orange pepper and cook, stirring frequently, for 8 minutes, or until the vegetables have softened.

3 Beat the eggs with the water and salt and pepper to taste in a medium-size bowl. Pour into the pan, add the broccoli and asparagus and stir gently. Cook over a medium heat for 3–4 minutes, drawing the mixture from the edges of the pan into the centre, allowing the uncooked egg to flow to the edges of the pan. Preheat the grill.

4 Sprinkle the top of the frittata with the sesame seeds and cheese and cook under the preheated grill for 3–5 minutes, or until golden and set. Sprinkle with the spring onions, cut into wedges and serve. Serve either warm or cold.

prepare in 10 mins
cooking time 25 mins
serves 2 – 4

ingredients

175 g/6 oz broccoli, broken into
    small florets

salt and pepper

85 g/3 oz asparagus spears,
    diagonally sliced

1 tbsp extra-virgin olive oil

1 onion, cut into small wedges

2–4 garlic cloves, finely chopped

1 large orange pepper, deseeded
    and chopped

4 eggs

3 tbsp cold water

25 g/1 oz sesame seeds

15 g/^{1}/$_2$ oz freshly grated
    Parmesan cheese

3 spring onions, finely sliced

Calories 221kcal	Fat 14.9g
Protein 14.1g	Saturates 3.69g
Carbohydrate 8.1g	Fibre 3.52g
Sugar 6.5g	Salt 0.31g

chilli bean cakes with avocado salsa

prepare in 10 mins +
30 mins chilling

cooking time 10 mins

serves 4

ingredients
25 g/¹/₂ oz pine kernels
425 g/15 oz canned mixed beans,
drained and rinsed
¹/₂ red onion, finely chopped
1 tbsp tomato purée
¹/₂ fresh red chilli, deseeded and
finely chopped
55 g/2 oz fresh brown breadcrumbs
1 egg, beaten
1 tbsp finely chopped fresh
coriander
low fat spray oil
1 lime, cut into quarters,
to garnish
4 toasted granary bread rolls,
to serve
SALSA
1 avocado, stoned, peeled and
chopped
100 g/3¹/₂ oz tomatoes, deseeded
and chopped
2 garlic cloves, crushed
2 tbsp finely chopped fresh
coriander
pepper
juice of ¹/₂ lime

1 Heat a non-stick frying pan over a medium heat, add the pine kernels and cook, turning, until just browned. Tip into a bowl and set aside.

2 Put the beans into a large bowl and roughly mash. Add the onion, tomato purée, chilli, pine kernels and half the breadcrumbs and mix well. Add half the egg and the coriander and mash together, adding a little more egg, if needed, to bind the mixture.

3 Form the mixture into 4 flat cakes. Coat with the remaining breadcrumbs, cover and chill in the refrigerator for 30 minutes.

4 To make the salsa, mix all the ingredients together in a serving bowl, cover and refrigerate until required.

5 Heat the oil in a frying pan over a medium heat, add the bean cakes and cook for 4–5 minutes on each side, or until crisp and heated through. Remove from the pan and drain on kitchen paper.

6 Serve each bean cake in a toasted granary roll, if desired, with the salsa, garnished with a lime quarter.

Calories 345kcal	Fat 15.9g
Protein 14.9g	Saturates 2.9g
Carbohydrate 40.5g	Fibre 8.4g
Sugar 7.4g	Salt 1.59g

warm red lentil salad with goat's cheese

1 Heat half the olive oil in a large saucepan over a medium heat, add the cumin seeds, garlic and ginger and cook for 2 minutes, stirring constantly.

2 Stir in the lentils, then add the stock, a ladleful at a time, until it is all absorbed, stirring constantly – this will take about 20 minutes. Remove from the heat and stir in the herbs.

3 Meanwhile, heat the remaining olive oil in a frying pan over a medium heat, add the onions and cook, stirring frequently, for 10 minutes, or until soft and lightly browned.

4 Toss the spinach in the hazelnut oil in a bowl, then divide between 4 serving plates.

5 Mash the goat's cheese with the yogurt in a small bowl and season to taste with pepper.

6 Divide the lentils between the serving plates and top with the onions and goat's cheese mixture. Garnish with lemon quarters and serve with toasted rye bread.

prepare in 15 mins

cooking time 35 mins

serves 4

ingredients

2 tbsp olive oil

2 tsp cumin seeds

2 garlic cloves, crushed

2 tsp grated fresh root ginger

300 g/10^1/$_2$ oz red split lentils

700 ml/1^1/$_4$ pints vegetable stock

2 tbsp chopped fresh mint

2 tbsp chopped fresh coriander

2 red onions, thinly sliced

200 g/7 oz baby spinach leaves

1 tsp hazelnut oil

100 g/3^1/$_2$ oz soft goat's cheese

4 tbsp low-fat Greek Yogurt

pepper

1 lemon, cut into quarters,
  to garnish

TO SERVE

toasted rye bread

Calories 422kcal	Fat 12.5g
Protein 28.1g	Saturates 5.4g
Carbohydrate 53g	Fibre 5.8g
Sugar 10g	Salt 1.77g

pasta with spiced leek, butternut squash & cherry tomatoes

prepare in 15 mins
cooking time 25 mins
serves 4

ingredients

150 g/5¹/₂ oz baby leeks, cut into
2 cm/³/₄ inch slices
175 g/6 oz butternut squash,
deseeded and cut into
2 cm/³/₄ inch chunks
1¹/₂ tbsp medium ready-prepared
curry paste
1tsp rapeseed or vegetable oil
175 g/6 oz cherry tomatoes
250 g/9 oz dried pasta
of your choice
300 ml/¹/₂ pint white sauce
2 tbsp fresh coriander leaves,
chopped, to garnish

1 Preheat the oven to 200°C/400°F/Gas Mark 6.

2 Bring a large saucepan of water to the boil, add the leeks and cook for 2 minutes. Add the butternut squash and cook for a further 2 minutes. Drain in a colander.

3 Mix the curry paste with the oil in a large bowl. Toss the leeks and butternut squash in the mixture to coat thoroughly.

4 Transfer the leeks and butternut squash to a non-stick baking tray and roast in the oven for 10 minutes until golden brown. Add the tomatoes and roast for a further 5 minutes.

5 Meanwhile, cook the pasta according to the instructions on the packet and drain.

6 Put the sauce into a large saucepan and warm over a low heat. Add the leeks, butternut squash, tomatoes and coriander and stir in the warm pasta. Mix thoroughly and serve.

Calories 291kcal	Fat 3.0g
Protein 11.9g	Saturates 0.5g
Carbohydrate 62.8g	Fibre 4.1g
Sugar 9.5g	Salt 0.25g

cajun chicken salad

1 Make 3 diagonal slashes across each chicken breast. Put the chicken into a shallow dish and sprinkle all over with the Cajun seasoning. Cover and refrigerate for at least 30 minutes.

2 When ready to cook, brush a griddle pan with the sunflower oil. Heat over a high heat until very hot and a few drops of water sprinkled into the pan sizzle immediately. Add the chicken and cook for 7–8 minutes on each side, or until thoroughly cooked. If still slightly pink in the centre, cook a little longer. Remove the chicken and reserve.

3 Add the mango slices to the pan and cook for 2 minutes on each side. Remove and reserve.

4 Meanwhile, arrange the salad leaves in a salad bowl and scatter over the onion, beetroot, radishes and walnut halves.

5 Put the walnut oil, mustard, lemon juice and salt and pepper to taste in a screw-top jar and shake until well blended. Pour over the salad and sprinkle with the sesame seeds.

6 Arrange the mango and the salad on a serving plate and top with the chicken breast and a few of the salad leaves.

prepare in 5 mins +
30 mins chilling

cooking time 15 mins

serves 4

ingredients

4 skinless, boneless chicken
    breasts, about 140 g/5 oz each

4 tsp Cajun seasoning

2 tsp sunflower oil

1 ripe mango, peeled, stoned and
    cut into thick slices

200 g/7 oz mixed salad leaves

1 red onion, thinly sliced and cut
    in half

175 g/6 oz cooked beetroot, diced

85 g/3 oz radishes, sliced

55 g/2 oz walnut halves

4 tbsp walnut oil

1–2 tsp Dijon mustard

1 tbsp lemon juice

salt and pepper

2 tbsp sesame seeds

Calories 425kcal	Fat 17.24g
Protein 52.3g	Saturates 2.12g
Carbohydrate 14.7g	Fibre 3.74g
Sugar 13.2g	Salt 0.67g

tomato, mozzarella & avocado salad

prepare in 15 mins
cooking time 0 mins
serves 4

ingredients

2 ripe beef tomatoes

100 g/3¹/₂ oz Mozzarella cheese

2 avocados

1 tbsp olive oil

1¹/₂ tbsp white wine vinegar

1 tsp coarse grain mustard

salt and pepper

few fresh basil leaves, torn into pieces

20 black olives

TO SERVE

fresh crusty bread

1 Using a sharp knife, cut the tomatoes into thick wedges and place in a large serving dish. Drain the mozzarella cheese and roughly tear into pieces. Cut the avocados in half and remove the stones. Cut the flesh into slices, then arrange the mozzarella cheese and avocado with the tomatoes.

2 Mix the oil, vinegar and mustard together in a small bowl, add salt and pepper to taste, then drizzle over the salad.

3 Scatter the basil and olives over the top and serve immediately with fresh crusty bread.

Calories 205kcal	Fat 17.4g
Protein 6.8g	Saturates 5.8g
Carbohydrate 5.5g	Fibre 3.3g
Sugar 5.0g	Salt 1.3g

tomato, **salmon** & prawn salad

1 Halve most of the cherry tomatoes. Place the lettuce leaves around the edge of a shallow bowl and add all the tomatoes and cherry tomatoes. Using scissors, snip the smoked salmon into strips and scatter over the tomatoes, then add the prawns.

2 Mix the mustard, sugar, vinegar and oil together in a small bowl, then tear most of the dill sprigs into it. Mix well and pour over the salad. Toss well to coat the salad with the dressing. Snip the remaining dill over the top and season to taste with pepper.

3 Serve the salad with warmed rolls or ciabatta bread.

prepare in 20 mins
cooking time 0 mins
serves 4

ingredients

115 g/4 oz cherry or baby plum
   tomatoes
several lettuce leaves
4 ripe tomatoes, roughly chopped
100 g/3^1/$_2$ oz smoked salmon
200 g/7 oz large cooked prawns,
   thawed if frozen
1 tbsp Dijon mustard
2 tsp caster sugar
2 tsp red wine vinegar
2 tbsp medium olive oil
few fresh dill sprigs
pepper
TO SERVE
warmed rolls or ciabatta bread

Calories 151kcal	Fat 7.4g
Protein 20g	Saturates 1.1g
Carbohydrate 1.2g	Fibre 0.3g
Sugar 1.1g	Salt 1.75g

roasted vegetable salad

prepare in 5 mins
cooking time 40 mins
serves 4

ingredients

1 onion

1 aubergine, about 225 g/8 oz

1 red pepper, deseeded

1 orange pepper, deseeded

1 large courgette,
about 175 g/6 oz

2–4 garlic cloves

2–4 tbsp olive oil

salt and pepper

1 tbsp balsamic vinegar

2 tbsp extra-virgin olive oil

1 tbsp shredded fresh basil

TO SERVE

freshly shaved Parmesan cheese

1 Preheat the oven to 200°C/400°F/Gas Mark 6. Cut all the vegetables into even-sized wedges, put into a roasting tin and scatter over the garlic. Pour over 2 tablespoons of the olive oil and turn the vegetables in the oil until well coated. Add a little salt and pepper. Roast in the preheated oven for 40 minutes, or until tender, adding the extra olive oil if becoming too dry.

2 Meanwhile, put the vinegar, extra-virgin olive oil and salt and pepper to taste into a screw-top jar and shake until blended.

3 Once the vegetables are cooked, remove from the oven, arrange on a serving dish and pour over the dressing. Sprinkle with the basil and serve with shavings of Parmesan cheese. Serve warm or cold.

Calories 190kcal	Fat 15.21g
Protein 3.7g	Saturates 2.59g
Carbohydrate 10.1g	Fibre 3.46g
Sugar 8.5g	Salt 0.06g

three bean salad

1 Arrange the salad leaves in a salad bowl and reserve.

2 Cut the onion in half lengthways, then slice thinly into half moons and put into a bowl.

3 Thinly slice the radishes, cut the tomatoes in half and peel the beetroot if necessary and dice. Add to the onion with the remaining ingredients, except the nuts.

4 Put all the ingredients for the dressing into a screw-top jar and shake until blended. Pour over the bean mixture, toss lightly, then spoon on top of the salad leaves.

5 Scatter over the nuts and cheese and serve immediately.

prepare in 5 mins

cooking time 0 mins

serves 4 – 6

ingredients

175 g/6 oz mixed salad leaves, such as spinach, rocket and frisée

1 red onion

85 g/3 oz radishes

175 g/6 oz cherry tomatoes

115 g/4 oz cooked beetroot

280 g/10 oz canned cannellini beans, drained and rinsed

200 g/7 oz canned red kidney beans, drained and rinsed

300 g/10$^{1}/_{2}$ oz canned flageolet beans, drained and rinsed

40 g/1$^{1}/_{2}$ oz dried cranberries

40 g/1$^{1}/_{2}$ oz roasted cashew nuts

70 g/2$^{1}/_{2}$ oz feta cheese (drained weight), crumbled

DRESSING

3 tbsp extra-virgin olive oil

1 tsp Dijon mustard

2 tbsp lemon juice

1 tbsp chopped fresh coriander

salt and pepper

Calories 301kcal	Fat 15.9g
Protein 16g	Saturates 5.6g
Carbohydrate 25.2g	Fibre 9.4g
Sugar 7.9g	Salt 1.29g

tabbouleh

prepare in 15 mins

cooking time 3 mins +
25 mins soaking

serves 4

ingredients

175 g/6 oz bulgar wheat

450ml/16 fl oz boiling water

8 vine-ripened tomatoes,
deseeded and chopped

7.5 cm/3 inch piece of cucumber,
diced

3 spring onions, finely chopped

4 tbsp chopped fresh mint

4 tbsp chopped fresh coriander

4 tbsp chopped fresh parsley

8 slices of Greek halloumi
cheese

DRESSING

juice of $^1/_2$ lemon

2 tbsp extra-virgin olive oil

salt and pepper

1 Cover the bulgar wheat with the boiling water in a large bowl. Stir and leave for about 20–25 minutes or until the bulgar is tender but still retains some bite. Drain well.

2 Transfer to a serving bowl and leave to cool slightly. Add the tomatoes, cucumber and spring onions and toss until combined. Stir in the herbs.

3 Mix together the lemon juice and olive oil to make the dressing and pour it over the salad. Mix well with a spoon, then season with salt and pepper to taste.

4 If serving with the halloumi, heat a griddle until hot. Place the halloumi on the griddle and cook for about 2–3 minutes, turning halfway. Serve the halloumi on top of the tabbouleh.

Calories 335kcal	Fat 14.58g
Protein 12.3g	Saturates 6.34g
Carbohydrate 39.9g	Fibre 1.94g
Sugar 6.3g	Salt 0.51g

bacon buns

prepare in 10 mins
cooking time 10 mins
serves 4

ingredients

8 low-salt lean smoked back
bacon rashers

6 tomatoes

250 g/9 oz low-fat natural
cottage cheese

freshly ground black pepper

4 large seeded wholemeal or
white bread rolls

2 spring onions, chopped

1 Preheat the grill to high. Remove any visible fat and rind from the bacon and cut 4 of the tomatoes in half. Place the bacon and tomatoes, cut-side up, under the preheated grill and cook, turning the bacon over halfway through cooking, for 8–10 minutes, or until the bacon is crisp and the tomatoes are softened. Remove the

tomatoes and bacon from the grill and drain the bacon on kitchen paper to help remove any excess fat. Keep the bacon and tomatoes warm.

2 Meanwhile, cut the remaining tomatoes into bite-sized pieces and combine with the cottage cheese in a bowl. Cut the bacon into bite-sized pieces and stir into the cottage cheese mixture. Season to taste with pepper.

3 Cut the bread rolls in half and divide the bacon filling evenly over each roll base. Sprinkle the spring onions over the filling and cover with the roll tops. Serve immediately with the grilled tomatoes.

Calories 263kcal	Fat 7.3g
Protein 19.8g	Saturates 2.7g
Carbohydrate 31.8g	Fibre 3.8g
Sugar 7.9g	Salt 1.82g

spiced risotto cakes with mango, lime & cream cheese

1 Preheat the oven to 200°C/400°F/Gas Mark 6.

2 Heat a large, non-stick saucepan over a high heat, add the onion and leek and cook, stirring constantly, for 2–3 minutes, or until softened but not coloured.

3 Add the rice and stock, bring to the boil, then continue to boil, stirring constantly, for 2 minutes. Reduce the heat and cook for a further 15 minutes, stirring every 2–3 minutes.

4 When the rice is nearly cooked and has absorbed all the stock, stir in the courgette and basil and cook, continuing to stir, over a high heat for a further 5–10 minutes or until the mixture is sticky and dry. Turn out onto a plate and leave to cool.

5 Meanwhile, to make the filling, mix the cream cheese, mango, lime zest and juice and cayenne together in a bowl.

6 Divide the cooled rice mixture into 3 and form into cakes. Make an indentation in the centre of each cake and fill with 1 x 15ml sp (1tbsp) of the filling. Mould the sides up and over to seal in the filling, then reshape with a palette knife. Coat each cake with breadcrumbs and arrange on a non-stick baking tray.

7 Spray each cake lightly with oil and bake in the oven for 15–20 minutes, or until a light golden-brown colour. Serve with green leaf salad.

prepare in 30 mins + 30 mins cooling

cooking time 45 – 50 mins

serves 3

ingredients

85 g/3 oz onion, finely chopped

85 g/3 oz leek, finely chopped

25 g/1 oz arborio or other risotto rice

500 ml/18 fl oz vegetable stock

85 g/3 oz grated courgette

15 g/^{1}/$_2$ oz fresh basil, chopped

25 g/1 oz fresh wholemeal breadcrumbs

vegetable oil spray

FOR THE FILLING

50 g/1^3/$_4$ oz 4% fat cream cheese

50 g/1^3/$_4$ oz mango, diced

1 tsp lime zest, finely grated

1 tsp lime juice

pinch of cayenne pepper

Calories 113kcal	Fat 2.5g
Protein 4.5g	Saturates 0.8g
Carbohydrate 15.3g	Fibre 1.8g
Sugar 4.8g	Salt 0.9g

raisin coleslaw & tuna-filled pitta breads

prepare in 5 mins
cooking time 5 mins
serves 4

ingredients

85 g/3 oz grated carrot

55 g/2 oz white cabbage, thinly sliced

85 g/3 oz low-fat natural yogurt

1 tsp cider vinegar

25 g/1 oz raisins

200 g/7 oz canned tuna steak in water, drained

2 tbsp pumpkin seeds

freshly ground black pepper

4 wholemeal or white pitta breads

4 dessert apples, to serve

1 Mix the carrot, cabbage, yogurt, vinegar and raisins together in a bowl. Lightly stir in the tuna and half the pumpkin seeds and season to taste with pepper.

2 Lightly toast the pitta breads under a preheated hot grill or in a toaster, then leave to cool slightly. Using a sharp knife, cut each pitta bread in half. Divide the filling evenly between the pitta breads and sprinkle the remaining pumpkin seeds over the filling. Core and cut the apples into wedges, then serve immediately with the filled pitta breads.

Calories 353kcal   Fat 7.18g

Protein 22.2g   Saturates 1.32g

Carbohydrate 52.9g   Fibre 5.25g

Sugar 10.0g   Salt 1.00g

desirable dinners

easy gazpacho

prepare in 10 mins +
2 hrs chilling

cooking time 0 mins

serves 4

ingredients
1 small cucumber,
peeled and chopped
2 red peppers,
deseeded and chopped
2 green peppers, deseeded
and chopped
2 garlic cloves,
roughly chopped
1 fresh basil sprig
600 ml/1 pint passata
1 tbsp extra-virgin olive oil
1 tbsp red wine vinegar
1 tbsp balsamic vinegar
300 ml/10 fl oz vegetable stock
2 tbsp lemon juice
salt and pepper
TO SERVE
2 tbsp diced, peeled cucumber
2 tbsp finely chopped red onion
2 tbsp finely chopped red pepper
2 tbsp finely chopped green
pepper
ice cubes
4 fresh basil sprigs
fresh crusty bread

1 Place the cucumber, peppers, garlic and basil in a food processor and process for 1¹/₂ minutes. Add the passata, olive oil and both kinds of vinegar and process again until smooth.

2 Pour in the vegetable stock and lemon juice and stir. Transfer the mixture to a large bowl. Season to taste with salt and pepper. Cover with clingfilm and leave to chill in the refrigerator for at least 2 hours.

3 To serve, prepare the cucumber, onion and peppers, then place in small serving dishes or arrange decoratively on a plate. Place ice cubes in 4 large soup bowls. Stir the soup and ladle it into the bowls. Garnish with the basil sprigs and serve with the prepared vegetables and chunks of fresh crusty bread.

Calories 128kcal	Fat 3.89g
Protein 4.7g	Saturates 0.57g
Carbohydrate 19.1g	Fibre 5.79g
Sugar 17.4g	Salt 1.61g

rustic roasted ratatouille

1 Preheat the oven to 200°C/400°F/Gas Mark 6.

2 Bake the potatoes in their skins in the oven for 30 minutes, remove and cut into wedges – the flesh should not be completely cooked.

3 To make the marinade, put all the ingredients in a bowl and blend together with a hand-held electric blender until smooth, or use a food processor.

4 Put the potato wedges into a large bowl with the aubergine, onion, peppers and courgettes, pour over the marinade and mix thoroughly.

5 Arrange the vegetables on a non-stick baking tray and roast in the oven, turning occasionally, for 25–30 minutes, or until golden brown and tender. Add the tomatoes for the last 5 minutes of the cooking time just to split the skins and warm slightly.

6 Mix the fromage frais, honey and paprika together in a bowl.

7 Serve the vegetables with a little of the fromage frais mixture, and sprinkled with chopped parsley.

prepare in 30 mins
cooking time 1 hour
serves 4

ingredients

300 g/10¹/₂ oz potatoes, scrubbed
200 g/7 oz aubergine, cut into
  1 cm/¹/₂ inch wedges
125 g/4¹/₂ oz red onion, cut into
  5 mm /¹/₄ inch rings
200 g/7 oz deseeded mixed peppers,
  sliced into 1 cm/¹/₂ inch strips
175 g/6 oz courgettes, cut in
  half lengthways, then into
  1 cm/¹/₂ inch slices
175 g/6 oz cherry tomatoes
0% fat fromage frais
1 tsp runny honey
pinch of smoked paprika
1 tsp fresh parsley, chopped, to garnish
1 tsp rapeseed or vegetable oil
1 tbsp lemon juice
4 tbsp white wine
1 tsp sugar
2 tbsp fresh basil, chopped
1 tsp fresh rosemary, finely chopped
1 tbsp fresh lemon thyme, chopped
¹/₄ tsp smoked paprika

Calories 200kcal	Fat 3.0g
Protein 5.8g	Saturates 1g
Carbohydrate 25.9g	Fibre 4.0g
Sugar 12.2g	Salt 0.06g

sweet & sour sea bass

prepare in 25 mins +
30 mins cooling

cooking time 15 mins

serves 2

ingredients

60 g/2^1/$_4$ oz pak choi, shredded

40 g/1^1/$_2$ oz beansprouts

40 g/1^1/$_2$ oz shiitake
mushrooms, sliced

40 g/1^1/$_2$ oz oyster mushrooms, torn

20 g/^{3}/$_4$ oz spring onion,
finely sliced

1 tsp finely grated root ginger

1 tbsp finely sliced lemon grass

2 seabass fillets, 90 g/3^1/$_4$ oz
each, skinned and boned

10 g/^{1}/$_4$ oz sesame seeds, toasted

FOR THE SWEET & SOUR SAUCE

90 ml/3 fl oz unsweetened
pineapple juice

1 tbsp sugar

1 tbsp red wine vinegar

2 star anise, crushed

90 ml/3 fl oz tomato juice

1 tbsp cornflour

1 Preheat the oven to 200°C/400°F/Gas Mark 6. Cut 2 x 38cm (15 inch) squares of greaseproof paper and 2 of the same size aluminium foil squares.

2 To make the sauce, heat the pineapple juice, sugar, red wine vinegar, star anise and tomato juice, simmer for 1–2 minutes then thicken with the cornflour and water mixture, whisking continuously, then pass through a fine sieve into a small bowl to cool.

3 In a separate large bowl mix together the pak choi, beansprouts, mushrooms and spring onions, then add the ginger and lemon grass. Toss all the ingredients together.

4 Put a square of greaseproof paper on top of a square of foil and fold into a triangle. Open up and place half the vegetable mix into the centre, pour half the sweet and sour sauce over the vegetables and place the sea bass on top. Sprinkle with a few sesame seeds. Close the triangle over the mixture and, starting at the top, fold the right corner and crumple the edges together to form an airtight triangular bag. Repeat to make the second bag.

5 Place onto a baking tray and cook in the oven for 10 minutes until the foil bags puff with steam. To serve, place on individual plates and snip open at the table so that you can enjoy the wonderful aromas as the bag is opened.

Calories 150kcal	Fat 3.0g
Protein 20.5g	Saturates 0.5g
Carbohydrate 28.0g	Fibre 1.5g
Sugar 15.8g	Salt 0.05g

fresh baked sardines

1 Slice 1 of the lemons and grate and squeeze the juice from the second one.

2 Cut the heads off the sardines and place the fish in a shallow, ovenproof dish, large enough to hold them in a single layer. Place the lemon slices between the fish. Drizzle the lemon juice and oil over the fish. Sprinkle over the lemon rind and oregano and season with salt and pepper.

3 Bake in a preheated oven, 190°C/375°F/Gas Mark 5, for 20–30 minutes, until the fish are tender. Serve garnished with lemon wedges.

prepare in 10 mins
cooking time 30 mins
serves 4

ingredients

2 lemons

12 large fresh sardines, gutted

2 tbsp olive oil

4 tbsp chopped
    fresh oregano

salt and pepper

lemon wedges,
    to garnish

Calories 352kcal	Fat 22.1g
Protein 37.3g	Saturates 5.7g
Carbohydrate 1.1g	Fibre 0.1g
Sugar 0.8g	Salt 0.55g

potato, herb & smoked salmon gratin

prepare in 25 mins +
20 mins cooling

cooking time 50 mins

serves 6

ingredients

400 ml/14 fl oz semi-skimmed milk

3 whole cloves

2 bay leaves

50 g/1³/₄ oz, onion, sliced

85 g/3 oz leek, chopped

100 g/3¹/₂ oz lightly cured smoked
salmon, finely sliced into strips

350 g/12 oz potatoes, cut into
2 mm/¹/₁₆ inch slices

2 tbsp finely chopped fresh chives

2 tbsp finely chopped fresh dill

1 tbsp finely chopped fresh tarragon

2 tsp wholegrain mustard

black pepper, to taste

35 g/1¹/₄ oz watercress

1 Preheat the oven to 200°C/400°F/Gas Mark 6. Line the base of a 19-cm (7¹/₂-inch) sandwich tin with greaseproof paper.

2 Pour the milk into a large, heavy-based saucepan, add the cloves, bay leaves, onion, leek and smoked salmon and heat over a low heat.

3 When the milk is just about to reach simmering point, carefully remove the smoked salmon with a slotted spoon and leave to cool on a plate.

4 Add the potatoes to the milk and stir with a wooden spoon. Return to a simmer and cook, stirring occasionally to prevent the potatoes from sticking, for 12 minutes, or until the potatoes are just beginning to soften and the milk has thickened slightly from the potato starch. Remove the cloves and bay leaves.

5 Add the herbs, mustard and pepper and stir well. Pour the mixture into the prepared tin. Cover with a layer of greaseproof paper and then foil and bake in the oven for 30 minutes.

6 Remove from the oven and place a saucepan on top. Leave to cool for 20 minutes before turning out onto a baking sheet. Put under a preheated hot grill to brown the top. Cut the gratin into 6 wedges and serve with the smoked salmon, tossed with the watercress.

Calories 107kcal	Fat 2.0g
Protein 8.5g	Saturates 0.8g
Carbohydrate 14.5g	Fibre 1.4g
Sugar 4.4g	Salt 0.9g

chilli chicken with chickpea mash

1 Make shallow cuts in each chicken breast. Place the chicken in a dish, brush with the olive oil and coat both sides of each breast with the harissa paste. Season well with salt and pepper, cover dish with foil and marinate in the refrigerator for 30 minutes.

2 Preheat the oven to 220°C/425°F/Gas Mark 7. Transfer the chicken breasts to a roasting tin and roast for about 20–30 minutes until they are cooked through and there is no trace of pink in the centre.

3 Meanwhile make the chickpea mash. Heat the oil in a saucepan and gently fry the garlic for 1 minute, then add the chickpeas and milk and heat through for a few minutes. Transfer to a blender or food processor and purée until smooth. Season with salt and pepper to taste and stir in the fresh coriander.

4 To serve, divide the chickpea mash between 4 serving plates, top each one with a chicken breast and garnish with coriander.

prepare in 15 mins +
30 mins marinating

cooking time 30 mins

serves 4

ingredients

4 skinless chicken breasts, about
140 g/5 oz each

1 tbsp olive oil

8 tsp harissa (chilli) paste

salt and black pepper

CHICKPEA MASH

2 tbsp olive oil

2–3 garlic cloves, crushed

400 g/14 oz no-salt or sugar
canned chickpeas, drained
and rinsed

4 tbsp semi-skimmed milk

3 tbsp chopped fresh coriander

Calories 321kcal	Fat 12.93g
Protein 36.8g	Saturates 2.09g
Carbohydrate 15.3g	Fibre 0.06g
Sugar 1.5g	Salt 1.04g

roasted squash wedges
with risotto & asparagus

prepare in 20
cooking time 25 mins
serves 4

ingredients

7 oz squash, peeled, deseeded
and cut into 4 wedges
1 tsp rapeseed or vegetable oil
100 g/3¹/₂ oz onion,
finely chopped
1 tsp crushed garlic
70 g/2¹/₂ oz three-grain risotto
mix (baldo rice, spelt and pearl
barley – available ready-mixed)
600 ml/1 pint vegetable stock
235 g/8¹/₄ oz asparagus tips
2 tbsp finely chopped fresh
marjoram, plus extra to garnish
3 tbsp 0% fat fromage frais
2 tbsp finely chopped
fresh parsley
black pepper, to taste

1 Preheat the oven to 200°C/400°F/Gas Mark 6. Spread out the squash wedges on a non-stick baking tray and roast in the oven for 20 minutes, or until tender and golden brown.

2 Meanwhile, heat the oil in a medium saucepan over a high heat, add the onion and garlic and cook, stirring, until softened but not coloured. Add the risotto mix and stir in half the stock. Simmer, stirring occasionally, until the stock has reduced in the pan. Pour in the remaining stock and continue to cook, stirring occasionally, until the grains are tender.

3 Cut 175g/6 oz of the asparagus into 10-cm (4-inch) lengths and blanch in a saucepan of boiling water for 2 minutes. Drain and keep warm. Cut the remaining asparagus into 5-mm (¹/₄-inch) slices and add to the risotto for the last 3 minutes of the cooking time.

4 Remove the risotto from the heat and stir in the marjoram, fromage frais and parsley. Season with pepper. Do not reboil.

5 To serve, lay the squash wedges on warmed serving plates, then spoon over the risotto and top with the asparagus. Garnish with marjoram.

Calories 121kcal	Fat 1.5g
Protein 7.5g	Saturates 1.68g
Carbohydrate 23.9g	Fibre 2.6g
Sugar 5.8g	Salt 1.73g

turkey with sun-dried tomato tapenade

1 Place the turkey steaks in a shallow, non-metallic dish. Mix all the marinade ingredients together in a jug, whisking well to mix. Pour the marinade over the turkey steaks, turning to coat. Cover with clingfilm and leave to marinate in the refrigerator for at least 1 hour.

2 To make the tapenade, put all the ingredients into a food processor and process to a smooth paste. Transfer to a bowl, cover with clingfilm and leave to chill in the refrigerator until required.

3 Drain the turkey steaks, reserving the marinade. Then heat the griddle and cook over a medium–high heat for 10–15 minutes, turning and brushing frequently with the reserved marinade. Transfer the turkey steaks to 4 large serving plates and top with the sun-dried tomato tapenade. Serve immediately.

prepare in 5 mins + 1hr marinating

cooking time 15 mins

serves 4

ingredients

4 turkey steaks

MARINADE

150 ml/5 fl oz white wine

1 tbsp white wine vinegar

1 tbsp olive oil

1 garlic clove, crushed

1 tbsp chopped fresh parsley

pepper

TAPENADE

225 g/8 oz sun-dried tomatoes in oil, drained and rinsed

4 canned anchovy fillets, drained and rinsed

1 garlic clove, crushed

1 tablespoon lemon juice

3 tablespoons chopped fresh parsley

Calories 366kcal	Fat 24.1g
Protein 27.7g	Saturates 3.5g
Carbohydrate 3.6g	Fibre 2.2g
Sugar 2.4g	Salt 1.46g

lentil bolognese

prepare in 25 mins
cooking time 20 - 25 mins
serves 4

ingredients

1 tsp rapeseed or vegetable oil
1 tsp crushed garlic
25 g/1 oz finely chopped
25 g/1 oz leek, finely chopped
25 g/1 oz celery, finely chopped
25 g/1 oz green pepper, deseeded,
finely chopped
25 g/1 oz carrot, finely chopped
25 g/1 oz courgette, finely chopped
85 g/3 oz flat mushrooms, diced
4 tbsp red wine
pinch of dried thyme
400 g/14 oz canned tomatoes,
strained and chopped (juice and
pulp reserved separately)
4 tbsp dried Puy lentils, cooked
to taste
black pepper, to taste
2 tsp lemon juice
1 tsp sugar
3 tbsp chopped fresh basil,
plus extra sprigs, to garnish
140 g/5 oz uncooked weight,
spaghetti

1 Heat a saucepan over a low heat, add the oil and garlic and cook, stirring, until golden brown. Add all the vegetables, except the mushrooms, increase the heat to medium and cook, stirring occasionally, for 10–12 minutes, or until softened and there is no liquid from the vegetables left in the pan. Add the mushrooms.

2 Increase the heat to high, add the wine and cook for 2 minutes. Add the thyme and juice from the tomatoes and cook until reduced by half.

3 Add the lentils and pepper, stir in the tomatoes and cook for a further 3–4 minutes.

4 Remove the pan from the heat and stir in the lemon juice, sugar and basil.

5 Serve the sauce with the cooked spaghetti, garnished with basil sprigs.

Calories 210kcal	Fat 2.0g
Protein 11.0g	Saturates 1.23g
Carbohydrate 42g	Fibre 4.4g
Sugar 6.9g	Salt 0.02g

roast beef salad

prepare in 10 – 15 mins
cooking time 45 – 50 mins
serves 4

ingredients

600 g/21 oz beef fillet, trimmed
of any visible fat
1 tsp pepper
2 tsp Worcestershire sauce
2 tbsp olive oil
400 g/14 oz green beans
100 g/3¹/₂ oz small pasta, such
as orecchiette
2 red onions, finely sliced
1 large head radicchio
50 g/1³/₄ oz green olives, stoned
DRESSING
1 tsp Dijon mustard
2 tbsp white wine vinegar
3 tbsp olive oil

1 Preheat the oven to 220°C/425°F/Gas Mark 7. Rub the beef with pepper to taste and Worcestershire sauce. Heat 2 tablespoons of the oil in a small roasting tin over a high heat, add the beef and sear on all sides. Transfer the dish to the preheated oven and roast for 30 minutes. Remove and leave to cool.

2 Bring a large saucepan of water to the boil, add the beans and cook for 5 minutes, or until just tender. Remove with a slotted spoon and refresh the beans under cold running water. Drain and put into a large bowl.

3 Return the bean cooking water to the boil, add the pasta and cook for 11 minutes, or until tender. Drain and return to the saucepan.

4 Add the pasta to the beans with the onions, radicchio leaves and olives in a serving dish or salad bowl and arrange some thinly sliced beef on top.

5 Whisk the dressing ingredients together in a separate bowl, then pour over the salad and serve immediately with extra sliced beef.

Calories 471kcal	Fat 23.1g
Protein 38.4g	Saturates 6.2g
Carbohydrate 29.2g	Fibre 5.0g
Sugar 8.0g	Salt 1.1g

blackened snapper with
sweetcorn papaya relish

1 To make the relish, place the onion, sugar, vinegar, sweetcorn, chilli, water, mustard seeds and turmeric into a small saucepan over a medium heat and bring to the boil. Simmer for 10 minutes, then add the cornflour mixture, stirring constantly, and cook until it is the required consistency (it will thicken slightly when cooled). Stir in the papaya and leave to cool.

2 To make the seasoning mix, put all the ingredients into a small bowl and mix thoroughly.

3 Sprinkle the seasoning mix over the snapper fillets on both sides and pat into the flesh, then shake off any excess. Lay the fillets on a board.

4 Heat a non-stick frying pan over a high heat until smoking. Lightly spray both sides of the fillets with oil, then put into the hot pan and cook for 2 minutes. Turn the fillets and cook all the way through. (If the fillets are thick, finish the cooking under a preheated grill as the less intense heat will prevent the seasoning mix from burning.) Remove the fish from the pan.

5 Add the lemon halves, cut-side down, and cook over a high heat for 2–5 minutes until browned. Serve the fillets, topped with relish, on warmed plates, with the lemon halves.

prepare in 20 mins +
45 minutes cooling

cooking time 20 minutes

serves 4

ingredients
4 snapper fillets, 85 g/3 oz each
vegetable oil spray
2 lemons, halved, to serve
FOR THE RELISH
2 tbsp finely chopped onion
1 tsp sugar
2 tbsp white wine vinegar
2 tbsp cooked or canned
   sweetcorn kernels
$^1/_4$ tsp finely chopped chilli
   or other type of chilli
100 ml/$3^1/_2$ fl oz water
$^1/_4$ tsp yellow mustard seeds
pinch of ground turmeric
1 tsp cornflour, blended with
   a little cold water
$1^3/_4$ oz papaya, cut into
   5 mm/$^1/_4$ inch cubes
FOR SEASONING MIX
$^1/_4$ tsp paprika
$^1/_2$ tsp onion powder
$^1/_4$ tsp dried thyme
$^1/_4$ tsp dried oregano
$^1/_4$ tsp cayenne pepper
$^1/_4$ tsp ground black pepper
$^1/_2$ tsp cornflour

Calories 134kcal	Fat 1.7g
Protein 17.4g	Saturates 0.3g
Carbohydrate 13.3g	Fibre 0.3g
Sugar 5.9g	Salt 0.28g

grilled tuna & vegetable kebabs

prepare in 10 mins
cooking time 15 mins
serves 4

ingredients

4 tuna steaks, about
140 g/5 oz each
2 red onions
12 cherry tomatoes
1 red pepper, deseeded
and diced
into 2.5-cm/1-inch pieces
1 yellow pepper, deseeded and
diced into 2.5-cm/1-inch pieces
1 courgette, sliced
1 tbsp chopped fresh oregano
4 tbsp olive oil
freshly ground black pepper
TO SERVE
lime wedges
selection of salads
cooked couscous, new potatoes
or bread

1 Preheat the grill to high. Cut the tuna into 2.5-cm/1-inch dice. Peel the onions, leaving the root intact and cut each onion lengthways into 6 wedges.

2 Divide the fish and vegetables evenly between 8 wooden skewers (presoaked to avoid burning) and arrange on the grill pan.

3 Mix the oregano and oil together in a small bowl. Season to taste with pepper. Lightly brush the kebabs with the oil and cook under the preheated grill for 10–15 minutes or until evenly cooked, turning occasionally. If you cannot fit all the kebabs on the grill pan at once, cook them in batches, keeping the cooked kebabs warm while cooking the remainder. Alternatively, these kebabs can be cooked on a barbecue.

4 Garnish with lime wedges and serve with a selection of salads, cooked couscous, new potatoes or bread.

Calories 352kcal	Fat 18.10g
Protein 35.8g	Saturates 3.36g
Carbohydrate 12.4g	Fibre 3.05g
Sugar 10.5g	Salt 0.20g

duck breast with noodles &
crunchy rice topping

1 Preheat the oven to 200°C/400°F/Gas Mark 6.

2 Put the orange juice, water, garlic, ginger, spices, orange zest and sugar into a small saucepan and bring to the boil. Reduce the heat and simmer for 3–4 minutes.

3 Lay the duck in a small, ovenproof dish and pour over the orange mixture. Cover with a tight-fitting lid or foil and cook in the oven for 1 hour.

4 Soak the rice in cold water for 10 minutes, drain and pat dry with kitchen paper. Heat a small, non-stick frying pan over a medium heat, add the rice and dry-fry until golden brown. Remove from the heat, tip on to one half of a clean tea towel, then fold the other half over the rice. Using a rolling pin, crush into fine grains.

5 Remove the duck from the cooking liquid with a slotted spoon, shred and keep warm. Transfer the cooking liquid to a saucepan over a medium heat. Gradually add the cornflour mixture, stirring constantly, and cook until thickened. Pass through a sieve into a bowl and keep warm.

6 Heat a wok over a high heat, then add the oil. Add the vegetables and stir-fry for a few minutes until cooked. Add the noodles, duck and sauce and briefly stir-fry. Serve in warmed bowls, garnished with spring onion and coriander and sprinkled with the rice.

prepare in 35 mins +
10 mins soaking
cooking time 1 hours
serves 4

ingredients
160 ml/2³/₄ fl oz freshly squeezed
  orange juice
200 ml/3¹/₂ fl oz water
2 tsp crushed garlic
1 tsp finely chopped root ginger
2 star anise
¹/₄ tsp sechuan pepper
2 tsp grated orange zest
1 tsp sugar
2 duck breasts, skin and any
  visible fat removed
20 g/³/₄ oz dry weight, white rice
¹/₂ tsp cornflour, blended with a
  little cold water
¹/₂ tsp sesame oil
100 g/3¹/₂ oz Chinese leaf, shredded
150 g/5¹/₂ oz beansprouts
150 g/5¹/₂ oz mixed deseeded
  peppers, finely sliced into strips
25 g/1 oz spring onion, finely
  sliced into strips
240 g/8³/₄ oz dry weight, egg
  noodles, refreshed in cold water
  and drained
FOR THE GARNISH
4 tbsp shredded spring onion
4 tbsp chopped fresh
  coriander leaves

Calories 388kcal	Fat 10.5g
Protein 22g	Saturates 3.1g
Carbohydrate 54.6g	Fibre 2.8g
Sugar 7.4g	Salt 0.42g

monkfish & asparagus stir-fry

prepare in 15 mins
cooking time 15 mins
serves 4

ingredients

500 g/1 lb 2 oz monkfish

4 tbsp vegetable oil

2 courgettes, trimmed, halved
and sliced

1 red pepper, deseeded and sliced

2 garlic cloves, finely chopped

150 g/5¹/₂ oz fresh asparagus
spears

100 g/3¹/₂ oz mangetouts

6 tbsp plain flour

4 tbsp lemon sauce (available
ready-made from supermarkets
and oriental food shops)

1 tbsp freshly grated
lemon-grass

1 tbsp grated fresh root ginger

salt and pepper

1 Remove any membrane from the monkfish, then cut the flesh into thin slices. Cover with clingfilm and set aside. Heat 2 tablespoons of the oil in a wok or large frying pan until hot. Add the courgettes and stir-fry for 2 minutes. Add the red pepper and garlic and cook for another 2 minutes. Add the asparagus and cook for 1 minute, then add the mangetouts and cook for 2 minutes. Transfer the vegetables onto a plate.

2 Put the flour in a shallow dish and turn the fish slices in the flour until coated. Heat the remaining oil in the wok or frying pan. Add the fish and stir-fry for 5 minutes, or until cooked to your taste (you may need to do this in batches). Transfer the fish to another plate.

3 Put the lemon sauce, lemon-grass and ginger in the wok or frying pan. Add the fish and stir-fry over a medium heat for a few seconds. Add the vegetables and stir-fry for 1 minute. Season, stir again and remove from the heat. Transfer to warm plates and serve.

Calories 253kcal	Fat 12.16g
Protein 23.1g	Saturates 1.54g
Carbohydrate 13.6g	Fibre 2.38g
Sugar 12.8g	Salt 0.07g

tuna & avocado salad

1 Toss the avocado, tomatoes, red peppers, parsley, garlic, chilli and lemon juice together in a large bowl. Season to taste with pepper, cover and chill in the refrigerator for 30 minutes.

2 Lightly crush the sesame seeds in a mortar with a pestle. Tip the crushed seeds on to a plate and spread out. Press each tuna steak in turn into the crushed seeds to coat on both sides.

3 Heat the spray oil in a non-stick frying pan, add the potatoes and cook, stirring frequently, for 5–8 minutes, or until crisp and brown. Remove from the pan and drain on kitchen paper.

4 Wipe out the pan, add the remaining oil and heat over a high heat until very hot. Add the tuna steaks and cook for 3–4 minutes on each side.

5 To serve, divide the avocado salad between 4 serving plates. Top each with a tuna steak, then scatter over the potatoes and a handful of rocket leaves.

prepare in 10 mins + 30 mins chilling

cooking time 20 mins

serves 4

ingredients

1 avocado, stoned, peeled and cubed

250 g/9 oz cherry tomatoes, halved

2 red peppers, deseeded and chopped

1 bunch fresh flat-leaf parsley, chopped

2 garlic cloves, crushed

1 fresh red chilli, deseeded and finely chopped

juice of $1/2$ lemon

low-fat spray oil

pepper

2 tbsp sesame seeds

4 fresh tuna steaks, about 150 g/$5^1/2$ oz each

TO SERVE

8 cooked new potatoes, cubed

rocket leaves

Calories 463kcal	Fat 24.1g
Protein 40.2g	Saturates 4.8g
Carbohydrate 22.7g	Fibre 4.9g
Sugar 8.3g	Salt 0.28g

salmon fillet with concassé tomatoes

prepare in 30 mins
cooking time 30 – 35 mins
serves 4

ingredients

4 salmon fillets, about
175 g/6 oz each, trimmed
1 tbsp olive oil
pepper
2 bunches asparagus spears,
trimmed
6 tomatoes, peeled, deseeded
and chopped
1 tbsp chopped fresh dill
grated rind of 1 lemon

1 Preheat the oven to 190°C/375°F/Gas Mark 5. Place the fillets on a chopping board and drizzle with a little oil. Season to taste with pepper. Heat a frying pan and fry the fish, non-skin-side down first, until browned. Turn over to brown the other side. Transfer the fish to a roasting tin and cook in the oven for 10–12 minutes, until the fish flakes easily.Melt the butter in a small saucepan, then leave to separate. Pour off the clear, clarified butter into a separate saucepan, and discard the white salty residue.

2 Cook the asparagus for 2–3 minutes in boiling water. Drain, rinse under cold running water, drain again and reserve.

3 Add the tomatoes, dill and lemon rind to a bowl and mix. Divide the asparagus and salmon between 4 plates, spoon some of the tomato dressing over each one and serve.

Calories 380kcal	Fat 22.8g
Protein 38.5g	Saturates 3.9g
Carbohydrate 5.5g	Fibre 2.6g
Sugar 5.4g	Salt 0.23g

sweetcorn & green bean-filled
jacket sweet potatoes

1 Preheat the oven to 190°C/375°F/Gas Mark 5. Scrub the sweet potatoes and pierce the skin of each potato with a sharp knife several times. Arrange on a baking sheet and bake in the preheated oven for 1–1¼ hours, or until soft and tender when pierced with the point of a sharp knife. Keep warm.

2 When the potatoes are cooked, bring a saucepan of water to the boil, add the broad beans and sweetcorn and return to the boil. Reduce the heat, cover and simmer for 5 minutes. Trim the green beans, cut in half and add to the saucepan. Return to the boil, then reduce the heat, cover and simmer for 3 minutes, or until the green beans are just tender.

3 Blend the oil with the vinegar in a small bowl and season to taste with pepper. Drain the sweetcorn and beans, return to the saucepan, add the tomatoes and pour the dressing over. Add the torn basil leaves and mix well.

4 Remove the sweet potatoes from the oven, cut in half lengthways and open up. Divide the sweetcorn and bean filling between the potatoes and serve immediately, garnished with basil leaves.

prepare in 10 mins
cooking time
1 hr 25 mins
serves 4

ingredients

4 red-fleshed sweet potatoes,
   about 250 g/9 oz each

115 g/4 oz frozen broad beans

115 g/4 oz frozen sweetcorn kernels

115 g/4 oz fine long green beans

140 g/5 oz fresh tomatoes, chopped

1 tbsp olive oil

1 tbsp balsamic vinegar

freshly ground black pepper

2 tbsp torn fresh basil leaves,
   plus extra leaves to garnish

Calories 360kcal	Fat 5.81g
Protein 11.2g	Saturates 1.04g
Carbohydrate 70.3g	Fibre 14.67g
Sugar 22.7g	Salt 0.26g

stuffed vegetables

prepare in 10 mins
cooking time 25 mins
serves 2 – 4

ingredients

2 medium aubergines.

2 tbsp vegetable stock

1 small onion, chopped

2 cloves garlic, crushed

1 tbsp tomato purée

6 ripe tomatoes, skinned and
chopped

4 tbsp cooked brown rice

25 g/1 oz pine nuts, lightly
toasted

1 tbsp chopped fresh parsley

1 tbsp chopped fresh mint

1 tbsp chopped fresh basil

$1/4$ tsp ground cinnamon

juice of 1 lemon

black pepper

1 Preheat the oven to 180°C/350°F (Gas Mark 4). If stuffing aubergines or courgettes, trim the stems, then halve lengthways. Use a teaspoon to hollow out each half, leaving a shell about 1 cm ($1/2$ in) thick. Chop the scooped-out flesh. Steam the shells over boiling water for about 4 minutes, then hold under cold water to stop further cooking and dry with kitchen paper. Mist the insides with oil-and-water spray. If stuffing peppers, slice off the tops (put to one side) and scoop out and discard the seeds. If stuffing tomatoes, slice off the tops (put to one side) and scoop out the seeds and flesh, and add the latter to the rice mixture in step 2.

2 Heat the stock in a frying pan, add the onions and garlic and sauté, stirring, until translucent. Stir in the tomato purée, tomatoes, chopped aubergine or courgette flesh (if using), cooked rice, pine nuts, herbs and cinnamon and continue cooking for a couple of minutes.

3 Stir in the lemon juice and season with pepper.

4 Lightly mist a baking dish with oil-and-water spray. Stuff the vegetables with the rice mixture and put the lids back on the peppers or tomatoes. Bake for about 20 minutes.

Calories 189kcal	Fat 6.07g
Protein 5.5g	Saturates 0.74g
Carbohydrate 30.2g	Fibre 5.33g
Sugar 9.3g	Salt 0.13g

ratatouille

1 Heat the oil in a large flameproof casserole over a medium heat. Add the onions and stir for 3 minutes. Add the garlic and stir around for a further 3 minutes, or until the onions are soft, but not brown.

2 Stir in the aubergines, courgettes, tomatoes, bouquet garni, sugar and salt and pepper to taste. Reduce the heat to low, cover the casserole tightly and simmer for 45 minutes without lifting the lid for at least the first 15 minutes.

3 Taste, and adjust the seasoning if necessary. Sprinkle with the basil leaves and serve at once or leave to cool.

prepare in 5 mins

cooking time
50 – 55 mins

serves 4 – 6

ingredients

5 tbsp olive oil

2 large onions, thinly sliced

4 large garlic cloves,
   finely chopped

350 g/12 oz aubergines,
   roughly chopped

350 g/12 oz courgettes, sliced

4 large beef tomatoes, peeled,
   deseeded and chopped

1 large bouquet garni of 2 large
   sprigs of fresh flat-leaf parsley,
   2 sprigs of fresh thyme and
   2 sprigs of fresh basil, tied
   together to a piece of celery

$1/2$ tsp sugar

salt and pepper

fresh basil leaves, to garnish

Calories 155kcal	Fat 10.20g
Protein 3.6g	Saturates 1.56g
Carbohydrate 13.2g	Fibre 4.25g
Sugar 10.9g	Salt 0.04g

tofu & vegetable stir-fry

prepare in 5 mins
cooking time 10 mins
serves 4

ingredients
2 tbsp vegetable stock
4 spring onions, chopped
2 cloves garlic, crushed
2.5-cm (1-in) piece fresh ginger,
peeled and grated
1/2 fresh red chilli, deseeded and
finely chopped
1 red and 1 yellow pepper,
deseeded and sliced
115 g/4 oz green beans, sliced
1 head broccoli, divided
into florets
115 g/4 oz beansprouts, rinsed
225 g/8 oz firm tofu, cubed
2 tbsp water
juice of 1 lemon
2 tsp sesame oil
55 g/2 oz blanched
almonds, halved

1 Heat the vegetable stock in a wok and stir-fry the onions, garlic, ginger and chilli for 2 minutes.

2 Add the vegetables and stir-fry for 3–4 minutes. Add the tofu and cook for a further 2 minutes.

3 Mix the water and lemon juice together, pour over the vegetables and cook for 1 minute.

4 Stir in the sesame oil and almonds and serve immediately on a bed of rice or rice noodles.

Calories 215kcal	Fat 12.91g
Protein 13.9g	Saturates 1.39g
Carbohydrate 11.4g	Fibre 5.92g
Sugar 9.1g	Salt 0.10g

chinese vegetables
& beansprouts with noodles

1 Bring the stock, garlic and ginger to the boil in a large saucepan. Stir in the noodles, red pepper, peas, broccoli and mushrooms and return to the boil. Reduce the heat, cover and simmer for 5–6 minutes, or until the noodles are tender.

2 Meanwhile, preheat the grill to medium. Spread the sesame seeds out in a single layer on a baking sheet and toast under the preheated grill, turning to brown evenly – watch constantly as they brown very quickly. Tip the sesame seeds into a small dish and set aside.

3 Once the noodles are tender, add the water chestnuts, bamboo shoots, Chinese leaves, beansprouts and spring onions to the saucepan. Return the stock to the boil, stir to mix the ingredients and simmer for a further 2–3 minutes to heat through thoroughly.

4 Carefully drain off 300 ml/10 fl oz of the stock into a small heatproof jug and reserve. Drain and discard any remaining stock and turn the noodles and vegetables into a warmed serving dish. Quickly mix the soy sauce with the reserved stock and pour over the noodles and vegetables. Season to taste with pepper and serve immediately.

prepare in 10 mins
cooking time 20 mins
serves 4

ingredients
1.2 litres/2 pints vegetable stock
1 garlic clove, crushed
1-cm/$\frac{1}{2}$-inch piece fresh
    root ginger, finely chopped
225 g/8 oz dried medium
    egg noodles
1 red pepper, deseeded and sliced
85 g/3 oz frozen peas
115 g/4 oz broccoli florets
85 g/3 oz shiitake
    mushrooms, sliced
2 tbsp sesame seeds
225 g/8 oz canned water chestnuts,
    drained and halved
225 g/8 oz canned bamboo
    shoots, drained
280 g/10 oz Chinese
    leaves, sliced
140 g/5 oz beansprouts
3 spring onions, sliced
1 tbsp dark soy sauce
freshly ground black pepper

Calories 353kcal	Fat 9.8g
Protein 14.7g	Saturates 2.04g
Carbohydrate 54.6g	Fibre 6.57g
Sugar 7.9g	Salt 2.34g

apple & plum crumble

prepare in 15 mins
cooking time 35 mins
serves 4

ingredients

4 apples, peeled,
cored and diced
5 plums, halved, stoned
and quartered
4 tbsp fresh apple juice
25 g/1 oz soft light brown sugar
TOPPING
115 g/4 oz flour
75 g/2³/₄ oz margarine, diced
25 g/1 oz buckwheat flakes
25 g/1 oz rice flakes
25 g/1 oz sunflower seeds
50 g/1³/₄ oz soft light
brown sugar
¹/₄ tsp ground cinnamon

1 Preheat the oven to 180°C/350°F/Gas Mark 4. Mix the apples, plums, apple juice and sugar together in a 23-cm/9-inch round pie dish.

2 To make the topping, sift the flour into a mixing bowl and rub in the margarine with your fingertips until it resembles coarse breadcrumbs. Stir in the buckwheat and rice flakes, sunflower seeds, sugar and cinnamon, then spoon the topping over the fruit in the dish.

3 Bake the crumble in the preheated oven for 30–35 minutes, or until the topping is lightly browned and crisp.

Calories 480kcal	Fat 19.0g
Protein 3.4g	Saturates 7.81g
Carbohydrate 79.2g	Fibre 4.42g
Sugar 41.4g	Salt 0.35g

mango cheesecakes

1 Line the base and sides of 4 x 150-ml/5-fl oz ramekins with greaseproof paper and very lightly oil.

2 Melt the spread in a small saucepan over a low heat, remove from the heat and stir in the ginger and oats. Mix thoroughly and leave to cool.

3 Using a sharp knife, cut the mango lengthways down either side of the thin central stone. Peel the flesh. Cut away any flesh from around the stone and peel. Cut the flesh into chunks and reserve 115 g/4 oz. Put the remaining mango flesh into a food processor or blender and process until smooth. Transfer to a small bowl.

4 Drain away any excess fluid from the cheeses and, using a fork or tablespoon, blend together in a bowl. Finely chop the reserved mango flesh and stir into the cheese mixture along with 1 tablespoon of the mango purée. Divide the cheesecake filling evenly between the ramekins and level with the back of a spoon. Cover each cheesecake evenly with the cooled oat mixture and chill in the refrigerator for at least 3 hours for the filling to firm. Cover and refrigerate the mango purée.

5 To serve, carefully trim the lining paper level with the oat mixture. As the oat base is crumbly, place an individual serving plate on top of a ramekin when turning out the cheesecakes. Holding firmly, turn both over to invert. Carefully remove the ramekin and peel away the lining paper. Repeat for the remaining cheesecakes. Spoon the mango purée around each cheesecake and decorate the top of each with 3 raspberries, if using. Serve immediately.

prepare in 15 mins

cooking time 5 mins + 3 hrs chilling

serves 4

ingredients

sunflower oil, for oiling

25 g/1 oz polyunsaturated spread

1/2 tsp ground ginger

55 g/2 oz porridge oats

1 large ripe mango, about 600 g/1 lb 5 oz

250 g/9 oz virtually fat-free quark soft cheese

100 g/3 1/2 oz medium-fat soft cheese

12 raspberries, to decorate (optional)

Calories 287kcal	Fat 14.58g
Protein 12.9g	Saturates 5.79g
Carbohydrate 27.9g	Fibre 3.84g
Sugar 17.4g	Salt 0.33g

blueberry fools

ingredients

25 g/1 oz custard powder

300 ml/10 fl oz skimmed
or semi-skimmed milk

2 tbsp caster sugar

150 g/5^1/$_2$ oz fresh or frozen
blueberries, thawed if frozen

200 g/7 oz low-fat natural
fromage frais

1 Blend the custard powder with 50 ml/2 fl oz of the milk in a heatproof bowl. Bring the remaining milk to the boil in a small saucepan and pour over the custard mixture, mixing well. Return the custard to the saucepan and return to the boil over medium–low heat, stirring constantly, until thickened. Pour the custard into the bowl and sprinkle the sugar over the top of the custard to prevent a skin forming. Cover and leave to cool completely.

2 Reserve 12 blueberries for decoration. Put the remaining blueberries and cold custard into a blender and process until smooth.

3 Spoon the fromage frais and blueberry mixture in alternate layers into 4 tall glasses. Decorate with the reserved blueberries and serve immediately.

Calories 136kcal	Fat 1.42g
Protein 6.8g	Saturates 0.86g
Carbohydrate 25.7g	Fibre 1.36g
Sugar 19.9g	Salt 0.18g

strawberry mousse

1 Drain the tofu and place in a food processor or blender.

2 Roughly chop the strawberries and put in the food processor. Reserve some of the orange zest strips for decoration, and put the remaining zest in the food processor with the honey.

3 Process until smooth, spoon into dessert dishes and chill in the refrigerator.

4 Decorate with the reserved orange zest.

prepare in 5 mins + chilling

cooking time 0 mins

serves 4

ingredients

225 g/8 oz silken tofu

450 g/1 lb ripe strawberries, hulled, washed and dried

zest of 1 orange

1 tsp honey

Calories 77kcal	Fat 2.48g
Protein 5.5g	Saturates 0.28g
Carbohydrate 8.7g	Fibre 1.24g
Sugar 8.5g	Salt 0.02g

healthier treats

summer fruit slush

prepare in 5 mins
cooking time 0 mins
serves 2

ingredients

4 tbsp orange juice

1 tbsp lime juice

100 ml/3¹/₂ fl oz sparkling water

350 g/12 oz frozen summer fruits
(such as blueberries,
raspberries, blackberries and
strawberries)

4 ice cubes

DECORATION

fresh whole raspberries and
blackberries on a cocktail stick

1 Pour the orange juice, lime juice and sparkling water into a food processor and process gently until combined.

2 Add the summer fruits and ice cubes and process until a slushy consistency has been reached.

3 Pour the mixture into glasses, decorate with whole raspberries and blackberries on cocktail sticks and serve.

Calories 59kcal	Fat 0.21g
Protein 1.6g	Saturates 0.00g
Carbohydrate 13.3g	Fibre 1.96g
Sugar 13.3g	Salt 0.03g

banana & strawberry smoothie

1 Put the banana, strawberries and yogurt into a blender and process for a few seconds until smooth.

2 Pour into a glass and serve immediately.

prepare in 5 mins
cooking time 0 mins
serves 1

ingredients

1 banana, sliced

85 g/3 oz fresh strawberries, hulled

150 g/5$^{1}/_{2}$ oz low-fat natural yogurt

Calories 202kcal	Fat 1.89g
Protein 9.1g	Saturates 1.09g
Carbohydrate 39.4g	Fibre 2.04g
Sugar 36.7g	Salt 0.26g

mixed vegetable bruschetta

prepare in 15 mins
cooking time 10 mins
serves 4

ingredients

olive oil, for brushing and
drizzling
1 red pepper, halved and
deseeded
1 orange pepper, halved and
deseeded
4 thick slices baguette or
ciabatta
1 red onion, sliced
1 fennel bulb, sliced
2 courgettes, sliced diagonally
2 garlic cloves, halved
1 tomato, halved
salt and pepper
fresh sage leaves, to garnish

1 Brush the grill with oil and preheat. Cut each pepper half lengthways into 4 strips. Toast the bread slices on both sides in a toaster or under a conventional grill.

2 When the grill is hot add the peppers and fennel and cook for 4 minutes, then add the onion and courgettes and cook for a further 5 minutes until all the vegetables are tender but still with a slight 'bite'. If necessary, cook the vegetables in 2 batches, as they should be placed on the grill in a single layer.

3 Meanwhile, rub the garlic halves over the toasts, then rub them with the tomato halves. Place on warm plates. Pile the grilled vegetables on top of the toasts, drizzle with olive oil and season with salt and pepper. Garnish with sage leaves and serve warm.

Calories 242kcal	Fat 10.54g
Protein 7.3g	Saturates 1.52g
Carbohydrate 31.6g	Fibre 5.29g
Sugar 10.6g	Salt 0.58g

mixed sushi rolls

1 Put the rice into a saucepan and cover with cold water. Bring to the boil, then reduce the heat, cover and simmer for 15–20 minutes, or until the rice is tender and the water has been absorbed. Drain if necessary and transfer to a bowl. Mix the vinegar, sugar and salt together, then, using a spatula, stir well into the rice. Cover with a damp cloth and leave to cool.

2 To make the rolls, lay a clean bamboo mat over a chopping board. Lay a sheet of nori, shiny side-down, on the mat. Spread a quarter of the rice mixture over the nori, using wet fingers to press it down evenly, leaving a 1-cm/$\frac{1}{2}$-inch margin at the top and bottom.

3 For smoked salmon and cucumber rolls, lay the salmon over the rice and arrange the cucumber in a line across the centre. For the prawn rolls, lay the prawns and avocado in a line across the centre.

4 Carefully hold the nearest edge of the mat, then, using the mat as a guide, roll up the nori tightly to make a neat tube of rice enclosing the filling. Seal the uncovered edge with a little water, then roll the sushi off the mat. Repeat to make 3 more rolls – you need 2 salmon and cucumber and 2 prawn and avocado in total.

5 Using a wet knife, cut each roll into 8 pieces and stand upright on a platter. Wipe and rinse the knife between cuts to prevent the rice from sticking. Serve the rolls with wasabi, tamari and pickled ginger.

prepare in 20 mins
cooking time 25 mins + cooling
serve 4 as a snack

ingredients

4 sheets nori (seaweed) for rolling
RICE
250 g/9 oz sushi rice
2 tbsp rice vinegar
1 tsp caster sugar
$\frac{1}{2}$ tsp salt
FILLINGS
50 g/1$\frac{3}{4}$ oz smoked salmon
4-cm/1$\frac{1}{2}$-inch piece cucumber, peeled, deseeded and cut into matchsticks
40 g/1$\frac{1}{2}$ oz cooked peeled prawns
1 small avocado, stoned, peeled, thinly sliced and tossed in lemon juice
TO SERVE
wasabi (Japanese horseradish sauce)
tamari (wheat-free soy sauce)
pink pickled ginger

Calories 326kcal	Fat 7.52g
Protein 13.8g	Saturates 1.32g
Carbohydrate 48.8g	Fibre 5.44g
Sugar 1.6g	Salt 0.63g

quick mackerel pâté

prepare in 10 mins +
chilling

cooking time 0 mins

serves 4

ingredients

250 g/9 oz skinless smoked
mackerel fillets
150 g/5¹/₂ oz low-fat natural
yogurt
1 tbsp chopped fresh parsley
1 tbsp lemon juice
finely grated rind of ¹/₂ lemon
freshly ground black pepper
TO GARNISH
4 lemon wedges
few sprigs of fresh parsley
TO SERVE
1 red pepper, deseeded and cut
into chunky strips
1 yellow pepper, deseeded and
cut into chunky strips
2 carrots, cut into strips
2 celery sticks, cut into strips
slices wholemeal or white bread,
toasted and cut into triangles

1 Remove and discard any remaining bones from the mackerel fillets and put the fish into a small bowl. Mash the fish with a fork and combine with the yogurt, parsley and lemon juice and rind. Season to taste with pepper.

2 Divide the pâté between 4 ramekins. Cover and refrigerate until required or serve immediately.

3 To serve, garnish the pâté with lemon wedges and parsley sprigs and serve with the prepared vegetables and toasted bread.

Calories 281kcal	Fat 20.09g
Protein 14.8g	Saturates 4.27g
Carbohydrate 10.8g	Fibre 2.49g
Sugar 10.3g	Salt 1.31g

tzatzíki

1 Peel then coarsely grate the cucumber. Put in a sieve and squeeze out as much of the water as possible. Put the cucumber into a bowl.

2 Add the yogurt, garlic and chopped mint (reserve a little as a garnish, if liked) to the cucumber and season with pepper. Mix well together and chill in the fridge for about 2 hours before serving.

3 To serve, stir the cucumber and yogurt dip and transfer to a serving bowl. Sprinkle with salt and accompany with warmed pitta bread, if using.

prepare in 10 mins + chilling
cooking time 0 mins
serves 4

ingredients
1 small cucumber
300 ml/¹/₂ pint authentic greek
    yogurt
1 large garlic clove, crushed
1 tbsp chopped fresh mint or dill
salt and pepper
warm pitta bread, to serve
    (optional)

Calories 45kcal	Fat 0.78g
Protein 3.8g	Saturates 0.5g
Carbohydrate 6.1g	Fibre 0.2g
Sugar 5.7g	Salt 0.12g

sultana tealoaf

prepare in 5 mins +
1 - 8 hrs chilling

cooking time 40 - 45 mins

makes one 450 g/1 lb
loaf – 10–12 slices

ingredients

sunflower oil, for oiling

40 g/1¹⁄₂ oz bran flakes

115 g/4 oz sultanas

85 g/3 oz demerara sugar

300 ml/10 fl oz skimmed or semi-
skimmed milk

200 g/7 oz self-raising flour

TO SERVE

tea or freshly squeezed
fruit juice

1 Very lightly oil a 450-g/1-lb loaf tin and line the base with greaseproof paper.

2 Put the bran flakes, sultanas, sugar and milk into a mixing bowl, cover and leave to soak for at least 1 hour in the refrigerator, or until the bran flakes have softened and the fruit has plumped up after absorbing some of the milk – the mixture can be left overnight in the refrigerator.

3 Preheat the oven to 190°C/375°F/Gas Mark 5. Stir the flour into the soaked ingredients, mix well and spoon into the loaf tin. Bake in the preheated oven for 40–45 minutes, or until the tip of a sharp knife inserted into the centre of the loaf comes out clean. Leave to cool in the tin on a wire rack.

4 When cold, turn the loaf out and discard the lining paper. Serve in slices with cups of tea or glasses of freshly squeezed fruit juice. Store any leftover loaf in an airtight container and consume within 2–3 days.

Calories 161kcal	Fat 1.2g
Protein 3.6g	Saturates 0.41g
Carbohydrate 36.3g	Fibre 1.37g
Sugar 19.5g	Salt 0.3g

fruit & nut squares

1 Preheat the oven to 180°C/350°F/Gas Mark 4. Lightly grease an 18-cm/7-inch shallow, square baking tin with butter. Beat the remaining butter with the honey in a bowl until creamy, then beat in the egg with the almonds.

2 Add the remaining ingredients and mix together. Press into the prepared tin, ensuring that the mixture is firmly packed. Smooth the top.

3 Bake in the preheated oven for 20–25 minutes, or until firm to the touch and golden brown.

4 Remove from the oven and leave for 10 minutes before marking into squares. Leave until cold before removing from the tin. Store in an airtight container.

prepare in 10 mins

cooking time 20 - 25 mins
+ 10 mins chilling

makes 9 squares

ingredients

115 g/4 oz unsalted butter, plus
   extra for greasing

2 tbsp clear honey

1 egg, beaten

85 g/3 oz ground almonds

115 g/4 oz no-soak dried apricots,
   finely chopped

55 g/2 oz dried cherries

55 g/2 oz toasted chopped
   hazelnuts

25 g/1 oz sesame seeds

85 g/3 oz jumbo porridge oats

Calories 310kcal	Fat 23.41g
Protein 6.0g	Saturates 8.35g
Carbohydrate 20.0g	Fibre 2.82g
Sugar 12.8g	Salt 0.05g

carrot bars

prepare in 10 mins

cooking time
35 – 45 mins + cooling

makes 14 – 16 bars

ingredients

sunflower oil, for oiling

175 g/6 oz unsalted butter

85 g/3 oz light muscovado sugar

2 eggs, beaten

55 g/2 oz self-raising wholemeal
flour, sifted

1 tsp baking powder, sifted

1 tsp ground cinnamon, sifted

115 g/4 oz ground almonds

115 g/4 oz carrot, coarsely
grated

85 g/3 oz sultanas

85 g/3 oz no-soak dried apricots,
finely chopped

55 g/2 oz toasted chopped
hazelnuts

1 tbsp flaked almonds

1 Preheat the oven to 180°C/350°F/Gas Mark 4. Lightly oil and line a 25 x 20-cm/10 x 8-inch shallow, rectangular baking tin with non-stick baking paper.

2 Cream the butter and sugar together in a bowl until light and fluffy, then gradually beat in the eggs, adding a little flour after each addition.

3 Add all the remaining ingredients, except the flaked almonds. Spoon the mixture into the prepared tin and smooth the top. Sprinkle with the flaked almonds.

4 Bake in the preheated oven for 35–45 minutes, or until the mixture is cooked and a skewer inserted into the centre comes out clean.

5 Remove from the oven and leave to cool in the tin. Remove from the tin, discard the lining paper and cut into bars.

Calories 221kcal	Fat 16.75g
Protein 4.0g	Saturates 6.69g
Carbohydrate 14.6g	Fibre 1.72g
Sugar 12.1g	Salt 0.14g

index